Missouri Simply Beautiful

Photography by Scott R. Avetta, Charles Gurche, and Ruth Hoyt

FARCOUNTRY
PRESS

Above: In Franklin County's Shaw Arboretum. CHARLES GURCHE

Facing page: Coneflower blossom. SCOTT R. AVETTA

Title page: At Ste. Genevieve. SCOTT R. AVETTA

Front cover: Zanoni Mill, near Gainesville in the Ozarks. CHARLES GURCHE

Front flap: Ox-eye daisies. RUTH HOYT

Back cover: Sit a while on the store's porch in Perry County. RUTH HOYT

ISBN: 1-56037-183-8
© 2001 Farcountry Press
Photography © 2001 Scott R. Avetta, Charles Gurche and Ruth Hoyt
This book may not be reproduced in whole or in part by any means (with the exception of short quotes for the purpose of review) without the permission of the publisher. For more information on our books call or write:
Farcountry Press
P.O. Box 5630, Helena, Montana 59604
or call 1-800-654-1105

Printed in China

On a cold January morning I arose at five o'clock, early enough to reach Winfield on the Mississippi River by sunrise. Soon St. Louis was left behind, and I had entered a rural setting blanketed in fog. The crisp morning had left a shimmering frost on the plants and farmers' fields, complementing the snow-covered ground. In the distance, an occasional tree seemed to dance in and out of the fog.

In Winfield I sat in silence and gazed into the fog. From across the river I could hear the call of an eagle, and in the next moment he exploded from the gray bank of fog. He gracefully perched on a branch hanging over his fishing hole. As the fog began to lift, I noticed he was just one of dozens perched high in the trees.

I realized what Missouri is all about: a morning filled with the beauty of man and nature, a morning of being surprised by the magic that exists if you take the time to look, a morning of finding another gift that many would never expect here. In fact, Missouri has the second highest eagle migration rate in the United States. Because we are in the Mississippi flyway, we also see thousands of snow geese and other migratory birds.

Missouri is located in an area where many biomes meet and overlap. At one time the land was covered with seas, glaciers, prairies and forests, which accounts for the varied landscapes and species we see today. There are pockets of natural communities that seem to have been lost in time.

Missouri's geological characteristics also attracted the Osage Indians, French explorers, Civil War veterans and pioneers who set out with the goal of westward expansion. The state is full of towns that still hold the values and architecture of the past, which are as unique and varied as our landscapes.

So take the opportunity to slow down, get off the main highways, and travel over the rolling hills through the farmlands and around the next bend in the river. You will be taken back in time to enjoy the sights and sounds that can be found only in Missouri.

—*Scott R. Avetta*

I became fond of Missouri's landscape at an early age, with weekend trips from the Kansas City area to Missouri's Gasconade, Niangua, Current, and Jacks Fork rivers. These waterways were the perfect place for an introduction to canoeing and camping, rock collecting and cave exploring, and for appreciating the beauty of Missouri's undisturbed natural areas. Thirty-five years later, I still feel the draw to this region, to see the clear river sliding beneath rounded mountains, to walk the shady trails, and to hear the song of whippoorwills on a still summer's eve. Now I return to the hills with a large-format camera and attempt to put a bit of this passion down on film. For fourteen years I've wandered down trails and back roads in search of that slice of the landscape that might show the essence and soul of Missouri. The more I've come to know this landscape, the more there is to discover. Like scattered treasure, unique and little-known places keep popping up with every trip: secret glades, running streams, ancient forests,

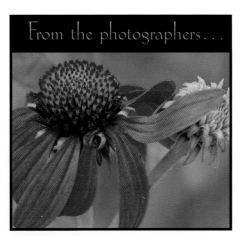

From the photographers...

gardens of ferns and wildflowers, rock sculpted into arches, knobs and pinnacles.

We owe much to the energies of those insightful people who have worked to preserve some of Missouri's remaining natural treasures. Many wild lands are now protected in state parks, wilderness areas, national riverways, designated natural areas, and private holdings. These lands provide a sanctuary for plant and animal life, and ensure that the special value of wildness will always endure in Missouri. Still, many pristine areas remain unprotected and vulnerable to destruction. Protection of the lands we are blessed with will preserve a quality of life for every following generation. Missouri's fragile beauty rests solely on our values and actions, for we are the stewards of a precious and irreplaceable landscape.

—*Charles Gurche*

As a long-time resident of Missouri, I know without a doubt that it is simply beautiful. I was truly startled when a non-resident friend told me that thinking of Missouri didn't conjure up thoughts of beauty and splendor. Perhaps this explains why Missouri bumper stickers read "Wake up to Missouri." With this book, these messages should be clear.

As a nature photographer I have learned to expect the unexpected from the natural world, and photograph what presents itself and speaks to me. The diversity of what Missouri has to offer causes excitement and anticipation preceding every trip, no matter where I go. You can explore the migratory birds' flyway and the Loess Hills in the state's west and northwest areas, or the lowlands and sloughs of the bootheel in the southeast. You can hike the trails of the blue springs of the south or the Ozark Mountains in the southwest, or the sand prairies in the northeast.

The purchase of my first camera opened the door to following my passion of spending as many hours in the day as possible in the world outdoors. As soon as I could leave the office I was on the road to somewhere else near or far, to enjoy and discover what subjects I could capture on film. No matter how much time was spent in the field, it never seemed to be enough. On more than one occasion, I delayed my return from an extended trip as long as possible to catch the last sunrise, and arrived back in town in the morning, just in time to return to the office for a full day's work.

Living in St. Louis presented many opportunities for learning about Missouri because of so many natural areas and resources nearby. I spent much of my time on the grounds of the Shaw Nature Center, interacting with its dedicated staff and volunteers who have helped preserve the beauty and essence of its native plant communities. These relationships expanded as I met and learned from conservation-minded individuals from organizations too numerous to mention.

My later move to South Texas filled me with mixed feelings. As much as I enjoy learning about the biodiversity of the Rio Grande Valley, I know that I must return to Missouri, my homeland, to reconfirm my passion for the beauty of this fine state.

—*Ruth Hoyt*

A classic country look in high-population St. Louis County. SCOTT R. AVETTA

Japanese red maple in the Missouri Botanical Garden, St. Louis. RUTH HOYT

In Ironton, St. Paul Episocopal Church's
neo-Gothic style dates from 1871.
SCOTT R. AVETTA

5

Visitors can enjoy this enchantingly rustic gazebo in the Whitmire Wildflower Garden at Shaw Arboretum, Gray Summit. RUTH HOYT

6

Right: Some days are better than others for mockingbirds. SCOTT R. AVETTA

Below: Composition in black and white at Whitmire Wildflower Garden. RUTH HOYT

Above: Focus on autumn at Grant's Farm in St. Louis County, once owned by President Ulysses S. Grant. SCOTT R. AVETTA

Left: Ha Ha Tonka State Park's namesake spring rises in the Osage River Hills near Camdenton. CHARLES GURCHE

Dairy cows go about their jobs in Hickory County. SCOTT R. AVETTA

Ozark National Scenic Riverways (portions of the Current and Jacks Fork rivers) were the first so designated in the United States; here flows Rocky Falls. CHARLES GURCHE

Herons are among the many waterfowl species that either migrate through or call Missouri home.
SCOTT R. AVETTA

Shaw Arboretum's Pinetum Lake in a mystic mood. RUTH HOYT

The Mississippi River, Gateway Arch, and city sparkle caught at dusk in St. Louis. SCOTT R. AVETTA

When Carthage rebuilt following its destruction in the Civil War, Victorian structures included Jasper County Courthouse, made of locally-quarried granite. CHARLES GURCHE

At today's George Washington Carver National Monument near Diamond, the Moses Carver home was built in 1881, when the future scientist was seventeen. CHARLES GURCHE

Patiently waiting for dinner to fly along. RUTH HOYT

Cypress reflections. RUTH HOYT

Missouri Town 1855 at Blue Springs takes visitors back to frontier days in a small town with costumed interpreters going about their daily tasks. CHARLES GURCHE

The morning sun throws chilly shadows across Sons Creek in Dade County. CHARLES GURCHE

Left: Maple seeds: a child's first helicopter.
SCOTT R. AVETTA

Below: Spidery tracery bejeweled with dew in Cole County. RUTH HOYT

Facing page: Sunrise over the Father of Waters, Missouri's eastern border. SCOTT R. AVETTA

Above: Wild hibiscus. <small>RUTH HOYT</small>

Right: Just waiting to be of service, in Miller County. <small>SCOTT R. AVETTA</small>

Facing page: Castor River flowing through Johnson's Shut-ins State Park, named for its many gorges, or "shut-ins." <small>RUTH HOYT</small>

Glad tidings of spring from a flowering pink dogwood. RUTH HOYT

Right: St. Louis symmetry. SCOTT R. AVETTA

Below: Site of St. Louis's original settlement, Laclede's Landing today is a historic district of shops, offices, and restaurants, and still a place to enjoy the Mississippi. SCOTT R. AVETTA

Above: Tulip time—upside down. SCOTT R. AVETTA

Right: The Carriage Barn at Watkins Mill State Park, Excelsior Springs, where a preserved 1861 woolen mill exhibits the equipment once used there. CHARLES GURCHE

Bald cypress trees rise from Otter Slough Natural Area. CHARLES GURCHE

On a tract of southern Missouri's eight-unit Mark Twain National Forest, bird's foot violets bloom amid oak leaves.
CHARLES GURCHE

Above: Untouched Ozark lushness at Shaw Arboretum. RUTH HOYT

Right: A snapping turtle's determined trek. RUTH HOYT

Facing page: Hodgson Water Mill in Ozark County. CHARLES GURCHE

In Squaw Creek National Wildlife Refuge, near Mound City. RUTH HOYT

The view from Illinois across the Mississippi River to St. Charles County. RUTH HOYT

Surrounded by signs of spring, Sandy Creek Covered Bridge near Hillsboro. SCOTT R. AVETTA

Virginia creeper and poison ivy—look but do not touch! RUTH HOYT

A spectrum of memories near Madison County's Mill Stream Gardens. SCOTT R. AVETTA

Visitors tour Elephant Rocks State Park billion-year-old granite on a gently sloping trail that includes the first self-guiding Braille trail in a Missouri state park. CHARLES GURCHE

Prairie sunrise near Gray Summit. RUTH HOYT

Quick-flowing waters in the Ozarks. SCOTT R. AVETTA

Dogwood heralds spring. SCOTT R. AVETTA

A liatris ladder for a monarch. RUTH HOYT

Above: Detail of St. Louis County's Old Courthouse, which was built from 1839 to 1862. RUTH HOYT

Left: Pelican Island Natural Area on the Missouri River gets its name from the Lewis and Clark Expedition, who were surprised to find pelicans on the prairie. CHARLES GURCHE

Sometimes photographers find images perfectly composed by nature,
such as this red maple leaf on a bed of star moss. CHARLES GURCHE

Dillard Mill, preserved in its namesake state park, ground grain from around 1900 until the 1960s, and has been restored to working order. CHARLES GURCHE

Left: In St. Louis's central west end, a castle arises. RUTH HOYT

Below: Fishing the Mississippi. SCOTT R. AVETTA

Facing page: An abstract view of Gateway Arch in St. Louis. RUTH HOYT

Left: Whatever does that human with the black box want? Meramec State Park. SCOTT R. AVETTA

Below: Historic Bethel was founded in 1844 as a communal religious colony. SCOTT R. AVETTA

The Norfolk River in Ozark County. SCOTT R. AVETTA

Missouri Town 1855's authentic buildings were moved here from around the state. CHARLES GURCHE

Aerial view of the Meramec River's rambles near Pacific. RUTH HOYT

Autumnal peace in Jefferson County. SCOTT R. AVETTA

Above: Flourishing on rocky soil. RUTH HOYT

Left: Arches over the North Fork on the White River in Mark Twain National Forest's Willow Springs Unit. CHARLES GURCHE

On Delmar Avenue near Washington University in St. Louis, Blueberry Hill displays the nation's largest collection of jukeboxes. RUTH HOYT

Above: Meramec State Park presents a bouquet of dogwood and redbud. SCOTT R. AVETTA

Below: Pike County's Clarksville lock and dam are ready to begin another day of Mississippi River shipping.
SCOTT R. AVETTA

Forest Park's 1,293 acres in St. Louis host many events. including this very serious rugby scrum. RUTH HOYT

Out for a spin in their pristine 1915 Model T, motorists pass Union covered bridge in Monroe County. SCOTT R. AVETTA

Two solemn residents of St. Louis's Soulard district. SCOTT R. AVETTA

Mist swathes the prairie at Shaw Arboretum on a muggy summer morning. SCOTT R. AVETTA

Above: Improving each shining hour. SCOTT R. AVETTA

Below: Cypress trees star in a study in lavender. RUTH HOYT

Above: The Red Mill in the Ozark National Scenic Riverways near Eminence served as a roller mill. CHARLES GURCHE

Facing page: Autumn color in Mark Twain National Forest. CHARLES GURCHE

On a unit of Mark Twain National Forest, oaks reach for the sky. CHARLES GURCHE

Change of seasons at Alley Spring, Ozark National Scenic Riverways. SCOTT R. AVETTA

Above: Reflections of St. Louis statue and the Old Courthouse in downtown St. Louis. RUTH HOYT

Facing page: A grove of Jackson County's eastern cottonwoods models winter dress. CHARLES GURCHE

Sandy Creek Covered Bridge in Jefferson County. CHARLES GURCHE

Left: Serving Zanoni Mill in Ozark County. SCOTT R. AVETTA

Below: Vernacular architecture provides a warm welcome to a St. Louis church. RUTH HOYT

Misty morning in Ste. Genevieve County. CHARLES GURCHE

Crabapples provide a fine snack for this cedar waxwing. SCOTT R. AVETTA

Flowers and lace, as arranged by Mother Nature. SCOTT R. AVETTA

Above: Looking westward across the Missouri River from Callaway County. CHARLES GURCHE

Facing page: Elephant Rocks with a crown of snow offer a scene of contrasts. CHARLES GURCHE

Above: Barns in Saline County settled for the night. CHARLES GURCHE

Preceding pages: Huzzah Creek Valley in Crawford County. CHARLES GURCHE

Mark Twain Lake surrounds the area where Samuel Clemens, the future Mark Twain, was born. SCOTT R. AVETTA

Tower Rock rises over the Mississippi River near Perryville like a ship's prow. CHARLES GURCHE

Beautiful, inviting, dangerous ice in St. Charles County. SCOTT R. AVETTA

Dewdrop diamonds shimmer on flower-petal fingers. SCOTT R. AVETTA

A window to learning at St. Louis University. RUTH HOYT

Designed by Eero Saarinen and completed in 1965, Gateway Arch rises 630 feet above
the site of the trading post that gave birth to St. Louis. CHARLES GURCHE

Above: Harvesting a hawthorne berry, this American robin is visiting Missouri Botanical Garden. RUTH HOYT

Right: Ste. Genevieve's Southern Hotel dates from about 1790. SCOTT R. AVETTA

Facing page: Wilson's Creek National Battlefield, near Springfield, tells the story of a battle in the fifth month of the Civil War. CHARLES GURCHE

View to a view of a view at the Castle, Ha Ha Tonka State Park. CHARLES GURCHE

Weston, on the Missouri River, boasts more than a hundred antebellum homes, and this period look downtown. CHARLES GURCHE

Right: Virginia bluebells surround a gentle waterfall in Washington State Park, near Washington. SCOTT R. AVETTA

Below: One of these battling bull elk probably wishes that Lone Elk Park, near Eureka, would live up to its name. SCOTT R. AVETTA

The castle at Ha Ha Tonka State Park, near Camdenton, began as a wealthy businessman's country retreat in 1905, later became a hotel, and burned down in 1942. SCOTT R. AVETTA

Left: Samuel Clemens lived at this white house in Hannibal from ages seven to eighteen; in the museum next door are Norman Rockwell paintings of episodes from his books. SCOTT R. AVETTA

Below: Power-breakfasting at a St. Louis hotel. RUTH HOYT

Facing page: St. Francis Xavier College Church on the campus of St. Louis University. SCOTT R. AVETTA

Above: Shaw Arboretum welcomes a soft summer day. RUTH HOYT

Facing page: Lush fields of southeastern Missouri. SCOTT R. AVETTA

Dogwood and maples wear autumn dress at Pickle Springs Natural Area, near Farmington. CHARLES GURCHE

Left: Missouri Botanical Garden, St. Louis, readies for winter. SCOTT R. AVETTA

Below: End of the line for the end of the train, at Hillsboro. SCOTT R. AVETTA

Güten morgen, near Hermann on the Missouri River. SCOTT R. AVETTA

Shortleaf pines, Mark Twain National Forest. CHARLES GURCHE

Above: Native Missouri wildflowers. SCOTT R. AVETTA

Right: Canyon on the Black River at Johnson's Shut-ins State Park. CHARLES GURCHE

Alley Spring in Shannon County. RUTH HOYT

Sweet coneflowers can be found near Gray Summit. RUTH HOYT

Right: Demonstrating its natural camouflage, a dragonfly. SCOTT R. AVETTA

Below: Survivor of many a season in Texas County. SCOTT R. AVETTA

Facing page: Rampart-like Buzzard Bluff looks down on the Sac River in St. Clair County. CHARLES GURCHE

Meramec Spring, the largest spring on the Meramec River. CHARLES GURCHE

Left: This northern fence lizard is a mama-to-be. RUTH HOYT

Below: Veterans of many a mile rest in St. Louis's Faust Park. SCOTT R. AVETTA

Above: After the ice storm, Squaw Creek National Wildlife Refuge. RUTH HOYT

Facing page: Winter slows, but doesn't stop, Grand Falls in Newton County. CHARLES GURCHE

This Warren County church, built in 1855, still functions without electricity. SCOTT R. AVETTA

Day's end near Cape Girardeau on the Mississippi. CHARLES GURCHE

The Grist Mill in Montauk State Park. CHARLES GURCHE

Twenty million gallons of water gush each day from Roaring River Spring over the waterfall above, at the Roaring River's headwaters. SCOTT R. AVETTA

Above: The reward for those who take the tram to the top of St. Louis's Gateway Arch. SCOTT R. AVETTA

Facing page: A much older arch, at the city's Washington University. CHARLES GURCHE

Above: Abstract beauty: dewdrop and coneflower petal. SCOTT R. AVETTA

Right: Awaiting a chilly dawn in Duck Creek Wildlife Area, Stoddard County. RUTH HOYT

Above: Many a young scholar has made this walk to Alley Spring schoolhouse in Shannon County. SCOTT R. AVETTA

Facing page: Meramec State Park receives the springtime benediction of a flowering dogwood. RUTH HOYT

Monroe County's rich farmland. SCOTT R. AVETTA

Lance-leaf coreopsis and gillardia. SCOTT R. AVETTA

The upper flow of Oregon County's Greer Spring. RUTH HOYT

Mating butterflies in Sach's Butterfly House in Chesterfield's Faust County Park. RUTH HOYT

Graceful tulip bud, Missouri Botanical Garden. SCOTT R. AVETTA

Above: Fog turns magnolia blossoms into an impressionistic scene. RUTH HOYT

Facing page: Signs of spring in Perry County. SCOTT R. AVETTA

Lake of the Ozarks, nicknamed "Big Dragon," has more miles of shoreline than California's Pacific Coast. CHARLES GURCHE